Baker Acted!
Three Days in a Mad House

by April Showers and Michael T. Sylvester

DORRANCE
PUBLISHING CO
EST. 1920
PITTSBURGH, PENNSYLVANIA 15238

Dorrance Publishing Co
585 Alpha Drive
Pittsburgh, PA 15238
Visit our website at *www.dorrancebookstore.com*

ISBN: 978-1-6453-0806-5

eISBN: 978-1-6453-0335-0

Foreword

Writing a book is not an individual endeavor. It takes many people, and I'd like to dedicate this book to all my friends and family who encouraged me to write my story. I dedicate *Baker Acted! Three Days in a Madhouse* to all the bipolars who struggle to stay in recovery and to the ones who are hospitalized and living on the edge. This book is for all the loving family members who want to understand the illness. This book is also dedicated to the psychiatrists, nurse practitioners, and mental health personnel who deal with bipolars every day. I especially thank Dr. Santosh Pillai for taking the necessary time to get to know me as a person, not just a patient.

My family, friends, and my Catholic faith have gotten me through the tough patches of loneliness and despair and the high times when I see the angels, Michael, Joan of Arc, Gabriel, and my Guardian Angel.

I want to thank my husband for showering me with faith, hope, and love. The greatest of these is LOVE!

I thank you for taking the time to read my story. Comments are welcome at april.showers@hotmail.com.

THE DOOR IS LOCKED. Like a half-broken hotel neon sign flickering on a dark highway, this is not a good sign. I press the intercom button 20 times.

"You can come in."

I open the dark door with hesitation. Why was the door sealed shut like a tomb? If it's locked, they either don't want crazies randomly coming in, or they want to keep crazies inside once they're in. Bad sign. The Ivy Green is supposed to be a friendly psychiatric hospital. That is what the colorful brochure says. Friendly psychiatric hospital. Oxymoron.

I walk in slowly like the drop of rain sliding off a leaf during a gentle storm and then thunder echoed. I walk in and click, so subdued intentionally, I suspect, so as to avoid suspicion. A click that inside my head shattered my serenity; don't they know my senses are heightened? Colors are brighter, sounds are amplified, at times, I can even see music, but still, the door locks behind me. Bad sign.

I walk across the polished floor that reminds me of a marine barracks just before an inspection. My image is reflected in the cat rim glasses balanced precariously on the tip of the nurse's nose as I go to the front desk and introduce myself. The room is painted the color of old urine, possibly to match the smell they are trying to hide with Pine Sol. It reminds me of what a cat owner will do before guests arrive.

"Hello. I'm April Showers. I was here yesterday and wanted to know if I could possibly get a copy of the psychosocial Melanie did on me yesterday. I'd like to have a copy for my records."

The receptionist looks dumbfounded. If I didn't know better, I would swear she was on lithium. Her tongue lashed out as she answered, "We don't do that."

My senses start to tingle as I spoke. My words are calm and clear but inside of me. I am composed, some may say overly confident, but I want the records.

I say with a glare, "Well, I'd really like a copy for my records."

She thinks she is clever, but I see her hand has moved under the desk as she asks, "Why were you here yesterday?"

She knows the answer, everyone knows the answer, she is stalling for time, but I don't care, so I answer with a grin like the one the Grinch had on Christmas morning.

"I came in because I'm bipolar, and August and September are my worst months for mania. I'm definitely elevated, on top of the world, and I just wanted to make sure I was doing okay. I was discharged as a patient from The Chateau because I wasn't the 'typical' patient. I was an outpatient there and got my meds from them. 'Typical' patient, they said I wasn't the 'typical' patient, and they discharged me like an old pair of sneakers that are missing one shoe. Now I'm back. I came here just to check to make sure I am okay. I know I'm okay, but I want to see in writing that Melanie said I was okay. So here we stand, waiting for a copy of the psychosocial for my records."

The nurse rises from the squeaky chair as if in slow motion. Her craggy voice is now becoming annoying to me as she says, "Wait here and let me get the nurse."

Get the nurse? I thought you said you were a nurse. More head games, more delay tactics, but I'm more focused now than when I entered this asylum.

Nothing is escaping my attention. Even the roach in the corner is testing me, evaluating me, wondering do I see him or not. The answer is simple. I do see the infestation, not just the roaches, but the decay of human spirit and compassion for mankind. This is where they want to send us. Not to help us, but to keep us quiet. Their blood boils like an active volcano when we are enthusiastic and passionate, and they sink into a world of darkness when we are quiet and no longer entertaining them.

Psychiatric nurses are the worst, always scary, but this is just my opinion or is it? You've seen Nurse Ratchet, the epitome in *One Flew Over the Cuckoo's Nest*. Jack Nicholson knew it. When psychiatric nurses talk to me, a small voice inside my head speaks the words, "And your little dog, too," but only I hear the voices. I used to like watching the *Wizard of OZ*. I even read the book during better times, but now I despise the concept. If the witch had her way, she would have locked Dorothy up. Sweet innocent Dorothy, simply because she was a dreamer.

The nurse comes out the thick wood and steel door quickly. On her face she wears her horned rim glasses and covering her slim almost sickly body is the white uniform. Are the glasses standard issue? I have not worked in years, and even I wear a pair of Vera Wang knock-offs. The nurse is unattractive, and the outfit made everything worse: 5'8", black, and athletic, looking like a 100-year-old marathon runner. She is serious and heading my way.

"Can I help you?" she hisses.

So, I have to repeat the whole story like an actress in a play that has been running for 20 years, a tale of being there yesterday and Melanie doing a 60-minute psychosocial on me, as if she didn't know this already. What, does she think I am stupid? I can see my name scrawled on the paper locked to the clipboard that she is ineffectively trying to conceal. Then I reveal what I should have known better than to mention, and Pandora's box is opened. The words trickle out of my mouth like a leaky faucet.

"I'm having some suicidal flashbacks. I'm not suicidal," I say in a rush, "but back in 2008, I was. I call these the 'dark times.' I'm bipolar and August and September are when the monster that waits under the bed, ever so patient, waiting for my worst months for mania to show itself to me." I look to the nurse who appears older and larger than when she walked in. Our eyes meet as I say, "I just want a copy of my psychosocial for my records."

Stepping closer, she asks, "How did you get here?"

"I drove my car. It's a Mustang Convertible, and it looks like the clouds are ready to burst with rain. Can I go put the top up?"

No response, only an eerie silence, the type of silence that you experience right before the scary part in a horror movie. What is she planning that my words don't register with this spiritless creature? Finally, after what seems like an eternity she utters, "You said you're having suicidal flashbacks."

The lid to the box opens a little more as I reply, "Yes, but I'm okay. Melanie said that it was normal."

"You drove here?"

"Yes, but my top is down. It's a convertible. It looks like rain. Can I go put the top up?"

"Why don't you come back here," meaning she wants me to go through the next set of locked doors. Bad sign.

"I told you. It looks like rain, and I have to put my car top up."

"Why are you in such a hurry?"

"My son starts swim practice tonight, and I have to be there."

"Why can't someone else take him?"

"It's going to be a family thing. I'm meeting my husband and him there."

"Call him and tell him you'll be late."

"He doesn't answer his phone."

"Call him."

I sigh, pretty exasperated at this point.

"I'll try, but he never answers his phone."

"Let me talk to him." Nurse Carol isn't getting it. I dial Mike's number and miracle of miracles, he picks up.

"Hello."

"Mike, I'm at Ivy Green, and Nurse Carol wants to talk to you. I told her I'm fine. I just wanted a copy of yesterday's psychosocial. Now they don't want to let me go without another. It takes an hour, and G has swim practice. The top's down on Kat, and they won't let me go put it up."

"Calm down. You're fine."

"Here's Nurse Carol."

"Hello. April says she's fine, but we'd like her to get evaluated. Can you take your son to swim practice?"

Not sure what Mike is saying. Hope he's not agreeing. I just want to leave and go have a smoke. I always smoke when I'm elevated. Calms me down. Slows me down. Saves my life from moving too fast. You move too fast, you make mistakes.

"Okay. I'll let you talk to her."

Nurse Carol hands me my phone. My lifeline to the outside world now that I'm locked in here.

"April," I hear Mike's voice, calm and cool. "You're fine. Don't worry about the car. I got it. Just do what they ask, and you'll be out of there. I got G."

"Okay, but make sure you get Kat's top up. It looks like rain. Bye, love."

"Bye, and don't worry."

Easy for Mike to say. He doesn't have the door locked behind him. Such a bad sign. Bipolars can read signs, and locked doors are bad signs. I'm starting to get nervous.

"How about I come back tomorrow?" I ask Nurse Carol.

"You have time now. Your husband has your son. Just come on back through the doors."

"Alright." No use arguing, although I do love a good argument. I'm hesitant as I glance at the double wooden doors, knowing once I walk through them, there's no turning back as they'll lock behind me. Okay. I can do this. I'm just elevated, but I'm fine. I'm antsy anyway and just want to walk. I go through the double wooden doors and click. They're locked behind me.

In the hallway is a lady waiting. Gray hair. Nothing ages a woman faster than gray hair. Doesn't she know that? She's older, but not wiser. I can already tell.

"Hi, I'm Angela, and I'll be your evaluator today. Just have a seat in here."

"Hi, I'm April." I sit down in the big leather chair. Tan. Couldn't they pick a better color? Or size? It's big, and I sink into it. They can try to make me feel small, but I've got my angels around me, and Joan is 10 feet tall. Angela sits across from me with papers on the table. "Can we do this outside? I really want a cigarette."

Angela gives a half smile.

"This won't take long."

Sure, her mind's not racing, and she's not the one locked in here.

"I'm not staying here," I tell her. She just stares at me. What's she thinking? Sure, they want me to stay. More money for them. But I'm not staying. I really want that cigarette. She starts asking me questions.

"What's your full name?"

"April Mary Showers."

"That's a pretty name."

"My mom's favorite season was Spring. And we're Catholic. So, Mary was a natural choice. My mom's name was Mary. Very Catholic. She passed away in 2010. Cancer. But she was 87. She was beautiful. People say I look like her. She could've been a beauty queen. A pin-up gal. I miss her."

"You're very pretty, too," she says this so condescendingly. I just stare at her. What's her game? "What's your birth date?"

"April 22, 1966. Kind of ironic my name is April, huh? Twenty-two is a good number. Runs in my family. My oldest sister was born on the twenty-second. She passed away in 2008. So sad. Only 58. Sudden heart attack. My oldest brother was born on the twenty-second. He's a good big brother. Looks out for me. My niece was born on the twenty-second. She's sweet. Her son was born on the twenty-second. My son was born on the twenty-second. Yeah, 22 is a good number. I'd really like a cigarette. There's a bench out front. Can we do this outside? I'd really like a smoke."

Again, she just stares at me. What's she thinking?

"This won't take long. I just have some more questions."

She's talking in slow motion. Can't she tell I just want to go? I'm fine. Just a little elevated, but I'm fine. Bless her soul, could she go any slower? I get my stress ball out and start squeezing. She looks at me.

"My therapist, Susan, suggested I use a stress ball to calm me down. My boy got this for me. Isn't it great?

It's a mini Earth. I've got the whole world in my hands. If I pass it from one hand to the other, it's supposed to get both sides of my brain working in synch. It helps. I have the number of my therapist, Susan Walker, on my phone. You can call her. She'll tell you I'm just fine. I just saw her Thursday. Do you want me to call her?"

I reach into my purse to get my cell phone, my lifeline to the outside world.

"The battery is dead. Do you have a charger? I have a car charger, if you just let me go out to my car. I don't have an electric charger. Do you have a charger?"

She looks at me.

"I'll check."

She gets up and goes across the hall to the office. It's got a half door. Kind of like a pharmacy door. She's walking in slow motion. God bless her. Where did they find her? I smile. I feel good. She said this won't take long, and then I'll be on my merry way. What's taking her so long? Cell phone. Charger. You either have one, or you don't. I see Nurse Carol talking on the phone. This leather chair is comfy, but I prefer to stand. I pass the ball from one hand to the other. She's still not back. I better go check on her.

I go across the hall to the half door.

"Excuse me." I see her in the corner sticking out from a partition. "Did you find a charger?"

"I'm looking."

Nurse Carol gets off the phone. I smile at her.

"We're looking for a charger for my cell phone. That way I can call my therapist, Susan, and this whole thing can be cleared up. But her number is in my contact list, and my cell phone went dead. Do you have a charger?"

Nurse Carol says, "I think we have one in here. Yes, here it is. Give me your cell phone, and let's see if it fits. I'll just plug it in here." Blip. There it goes. Alleuljah. That sound is music to my ears. Now it just needs to charge, and we can get Susan on the phone, this will all be cleared up, and I can go have my smoke. Praise the Lord.

Angela comes to the door and says, "Let's go back across the hall and finish the inventory."

"No problem," I tell her.

We walk back across the hall, and I sit down in the comfy leather chair, and she sits down across from me with the papers on the table.

"This is just a formality. If you can sign the bottom of this paper. It just states that you understand if you have to stay here, it's $500 per day."

"But I'm not staying."

"I know. It's just a formality."

I pick up the pen, hesitating.

"I know, but I'm not staying here."

"You said you were having suicidal flashbacks."

"Yes, but I'm not suicidal. I was back in 2008, but not now. But sometimes I get flashbacks."

"Did you ever act on them or were you hospitalized?"

"I was never hospitalized. It's amazing how the human mind wants to keep you alive. I get these flashbacks, especially when I'm driving over bridges. Back in 2008, I used to have recurring thoughts of driving over a bridge, giving one quick turn, and then it'd be all over. So now, sometimes when I'm driving over bridges, I get flashbacks. Melanie said that's normal, and nothing to be concerned about."

"Did you ever try to commit suicide in other ways?"

"Sure. Bleach and ammonia. Poured them together in a bucket and put a towel over my head and breathed in deeply. Nothing happened. I used to sit in my bedroom closet and put a bag over my head and tape it shut. Put my mouth up to the car exhaust in the garage with the car running. Tried to choke by stuffing marshmallows in my mouth. Chubby Bunny game. Saw it on Oprah. It can choke you. Got a hypodermic needle and tried shooting air into my chest arteries. Got a helium tank from the Party Store to go with the plastic bags. Tried stabbing myself. Crazy things go through your mind when you're in that state. Do you think my cell phone is done charging? We should check."

I get up and walk across the hall to the half door. Nurse Carol is on the phone again. I try to get her attention. I can see my lifeline on the floor charging.

Angela comes up behind me and says, "Excuse me."

I let her by me, and she closes the half door behind her. She checks the phone and hands it to me.

"Thank you," I say politely.

I walk back to the room across the hall and sit down in the comfy leather chair. This is such a blah room. You would think they'd at least put some pictures on the wall. All tan. Like tan is supposed to calm you down. Even the table is tan. And the pen black. Pick at least an uplifting color. Like purple. A purple pen would be nice. I used to use a purple pen all the time to grade papers when I taught elementary school. Very non-threatening. Or green. Green's nice. Then again, these are official documents. So black it is.

Angela comes back in. Bless her soul, she's slow. She sits down and smiles. As soon as she starts asking a question, I hear a man screaming, "Nooooooooooo!" Then I see four orderlies pushing an old man strapped to a stretcher past our door. He's trying with all his might to sit up, but he's strapped down. His blue eyes meet mine as I look at him and he at me. It's just a split second, but I see terror in his eyes. He's screaming, "Nooooooooooo!" and for an instant, we connect. He shouldn't be strapped down. He's harmless. I just know it. I can sense it. I sense his terror.

The orderlies just look at me. They do nothing. Just keep wheeling the stretcher. Can't they see he's terrified? Do they care? They look away and keep wheeling the stretcher. Then the old man is out of sight. I can hear him in the next room.

Angela smiles as if nothing just happened. Nurse Carol comes in. She shows a paper to Angela, and Angela gets up and says, "I'll just be a moment." She gets up and walks across the hallway and closes the door behind her. I feel confined.

I get out my cell phone and try calling Susan. It rings once. Come on, Susan, pick up. It rings again. I'm praying she answers, so this whole misunderstanding can be cleared up, and I can go and have my smoke. Third ring, and then it goes to voicemail. Shit.

"This is Susan Walker. Licensed mental health counselor. Please leave your name and number, and I'll get back to you shortly. I am currently accepting new patients." Beep.

"Susan, this is April Showers. I'm at Ivy Green, and they won't let me go. Can you call them and tell them I'm fine? My number is 352-552-2222. Thanks, Susan. Please call."

I hang up and slip the cell phone back into my purse.

With this door closed, I feel claustrophobic. I need air and just need to walk. I can't just sit here. Angela is so slow, God only knows when she'll be back. I grab my purse and venture into the hallway. I walk past the room next door and see the old man just sitting there. The door is closed, but no one else is in there with him. The stretcher is gone. I keep walking. I see a young girl who looks like Julia Roberts sitting with an evaluator in the room two doors down. I keep walking. I come to the double wooden doors I came through. I push. Wishful thinking. I know they're locked, but it doesn't hurt to have hope.

On the wall is an intercom. What would they do if I pressed it? Maybe think I'm a nurse and buzz me out. One, two, three, four, five times I press it.

"Ma'am, you don't need to press that," the voice tells me through the intercom. Oops. I look behind me, and they can see me from the front office. I'm tempted to try the office door, but I know it's probably locked. I turn around and go back the way I came. The girl that looks like Julia Roberts is still being evaluated. She looks very normal to me.

I look into the room where the old man is sitting. I hesitate, but then I know in my heart it's the right thing to do. I open the door and say hello. He looks up and says, "Hi," in a gruff voice that I know has just been screaming. His blue eyes look into my green eyes, and I know I have nothing to fear. He's harmless. I sit down at the table and introduce myself.

"I'm April. I'm in the next room getting evaluated, and I saw you being wheeled in on the stretcher. My evaluator is in the office, and I'm antsy right now, so I thought I'd come over here. I'm bipolar, and August and September are my worst months for mania. I came by yesterday, and they did an hour long psychosocial on me. She said I was fine. I came back today to get a copy of the psychosocial for my records, and now they want to evaluate me again. Angela's my evaluator. God bless her, but she's so slow."

"I'm Tom. I'm trying to make a phone call, but this damn phone doesn't work. I dialed, but it doesn't seem to go through." He seems very calm. "I'm the caretaker for my 93-year-old mom, and I have to get in touch with my neighbor to check on her."

"I have my cell phone. It's my lifeline to the outside world. What's the number?"

He gives me the number, and I dial it. I want to help this Tom. He seems perfectly sane and normal.

"Hello, Sally, my mom is by herself. Can you go check on her? I'm here in Ocala. They want to keep me for observation. Yeah. Thanks."

Tom hands me back my lifeline.

"Why are you here?" I ask him.

"Ah, damn. I went to see my psychiatrist at the VA clinic on Friday. I have PTSD. The psychiatrist, it was a new one, asked me 'Are you afraid to die?' Of course I said, 'No.' I was military for 20 years. No, I'm not afraid to die. Right away they Baker Acted me. Said I was suicidal. I live down near Tampa, but they didn't have any beds down there, so they brought me up here."

"Crazy," is all I can think of to say. "They just want to keep you here for the money."

"Damn, right."

"I'd expect any soldier to answer the way you did. Now you're stuck here for being honest. And you have to scramble to make sure someone watches your mom. That's just nuts."

"Yeah," Tom sighs, not too happy. Who would be?

I glance back and see Angela at the door. She's not too happy either,

"April, you can't wander around like this. Come back to the office now."

She's not smiling. I smile.

"Tom here, needed to use the phone. His mom's 93 and alone. I was just helping him."

"You need to come back to the office," she says sternly.

"Bye, Tom, and good luck."

"Yeah, you too."

I smile and get up and walk back to the room.

"Just wait here, and Nurse Carol will be in with the doctor."

"Okay."

Finally, a psychiatrist. Not a registered nurse or an ARNP, but a bona fide psychiatrist. He'll see. I'm fine and then I can get out of here.

I stay standing in lieu of the big tan chair. I know this'll be quick. I have my stress ball going back and forth. Back and forth. I move from foot to foot. I sure would love a cigarette right now.

I see Nurse Carol coming and in front of her is this tall, Indian looking middle-aged man. He's big, though. At least 6'2" tall and looks like he works out. Must have some African-American blood in him. But he's still Indian. He comes in and sits down at the tan table across from me. Nurse Carol sits down next to him.

"Hi, I'm April."

I extend my right hand out to him and smile as I shake his hand. Nice firm grip. Good sign, I think.

Then with his Indian accent he addresses me, "I'm Dr. Nadir. Have a seat." No smile. Seems so serious. I'm thinking, "Lighten up." He has papers in front of him.

"I prefer to stand. I'm bipolar, and August and September are my worst months for mania. And I'm elevated right now. I prefer to stand."

With the Indian accent in full force, he says again, "Have a seat."

"I told you. I'm a little manic right now, and I prefer to stand," I say with a smile. Then it popped out. "What, do you have a little OCD going on?" I joke.

He looks at Nurse Carol, annoyed, and says, "Baker Act her."

What? How could he say that? I was just joking with him. Was he that offended? He can't do this.

"Noooooooooo!" I yell. He quickly gets up, and Nurse Carol quickly yells, "Get security. Get security!"

I'm not sure what to do. No. How could he do this? No. I'm not staying in this nut house. No. I have to get out of here. I drop my ball and grab my purse and run to the double wooden doors. I push and push. Locked. I knew it was a bad sign.

I quickly get my cell phone out. Mike will never answer. Big brother. I'll call my big brother, Mike. I grab my lifeline and flip it open. Contacts. Scroll. Brother Mike. Send.

"Hello," I hear his voice.

I breathlessly say, "Mike, I'm at Ivy Green. The psychiatrist just saw me, and he said Baker Act her. I don't know what to do."

"What? I just talked to you and you were just fine. What's going on?"

"I don't know, but call my Mike."

Before I can say another word, Nurse Carol and four ex-military looking guys are headed towards me.

"Get the cell phone. Get the cell phone," I hear Nurse Carol bark.

"Nooooooooooo!" I scream at the top of my lungs. They're trying to get my cell phone. My lifeline. Can't let it happen. Two of the guys try to get it. I see the office door open to my right. I head straight for it before they know what I'm doing. There has to be a way out. I feel like a trapped rat. Where do I go? I squeeze in behind the water cooler.

"April, just calm down. We want to help you."

"I'm not staying here," I shake my head no.

They're all looking at me. They attempt to come closer, and I knock the water cooler down between us. I'm trapped. There's only a window behind me. They're all looking at me. I'm breathing heavy.

"April, just come out here and we can talk," Nurse Carol says. I clutch my lifeline tightly in my right hand. This is all a misunderstanding.

"Okay, but I'm not staying here."

I move towards them and the two ex-military grab my wrists and start walking me back to the evaluation room.

I hear Nurse Carol bark, "Get the cell phone."

The one ex-military looking orderly tries to get it, but I have a new burst of energy, and I quickly break free and run back to the evaluation room clutching my lifeline. I try to quickly shut the door behind me, but I'm not fast enough. The orderlies throw me up against the wall, my hands spread out. Still clutching my lifeline.

"Get the cell phone," I hear Nurse Carol order again. Why are they so worried about my cell phone? They don't want any of this recorded. That's it. They know they're wrong. What the hell are they going to do with me?

I squeeze my right hand free and impulsively go under my dress and slip the cell phone where only a woman can slip it. I have my Batgirl underwear on. I feel like a tortured superhero.

"Get the shot. Get the shot."

I turn my head and look straight into the black man's eyes and let out a shrill scream, "Ahhhhhhhhhh!"

The phone slips out. They start reaching around front. I quickly break my hand free and reach into my underwear, palm it and curl my hand around it.

Then my black cape dress is lifted up and underwear, too. Then, "Owwww! That better not be a shot of Haldol. That better not be a shot of Haldol."

They're still holding me.

"Calm down, April. Calm down."

I can't see much being restrained up against the wall. I try to break free. Four ex-military looking orderlies restraining me. Me! Little old me. What's going on? What do they think I'm going to do? Then I look to my right and get a glimpse of the orderly's pants leg, and I move so I can get a good shot. Then I pee on him. Serves him right for slapping me up against the wall.

"Get some towels. Get some towels," I hear someone yell.

"Get the cell phone," I hear Nurse Carol say. They finally pry it out of my hands.

"Okay. Okay. Just let me go," my heart's pounding.

Nurse Carol says, "Let her go."

I collapse to the ground.

"What did you shoot me with?"

"Just relax and let it work," one of the orderlies says. I see the wet spot on the floor and feel a bit of satisfaction. This is humiliating. I have to get out of here. I need the police or somebody rational. Somebody rational is probably better than the police. Me and the cops don't always see eye to eye. They usually view me as confrontational. I just like to state my mind, but they tend to view it as confrontational. So, yeah, somebody rational is a much better choice.

"This is all a mistake." I look at Nurse Carol. I snarl, "I thought you were here to help me."

"I am here to help you."

"What did you shoot me with?"

"Something to calm you down."

"What was it?"

She just turns and walks out.

The two orderlies and a nurse with a needle are at the door. They're joking about the weekend. Talking about how they went out. I look at the nurse.

"What's your name?" I snarl.

She looks at me and says, "Nikki."

I snarl back, "You're an ugly bitch."

She says with an attitude, "It'll be ugly when I shoot this in your ass." And she holds up the needle.

I step back and see the landline phone on the floor. I slowly step back and then a mad dash. Pick up. Dial 911.

"Help, help. They're keeping me here against my will. I'm fine, and they're keeping me here."

"Quick, get the phone. Get it out of the wall."

The orderly comes and rips the cord out of the wall and yanks the receiver from my hand. Damn. No lifeline.

"Take her to the back," Nurse Carol instructs an orderly who looks ex-military. He has on the straight-armed military issued glasses. I go, but he's still holding on to my arm.

"Was that Haldol they shot me with?"

"Yeah. The best thing to do is just let it work."

"Have you ever had Haldol?"

"Yeah, they used to give it to the soldiers in the tanks before going into battle. Just let it work."

"This is all a mistake. I'm perfectly fine. This is all a mistake. The psychiatrist just didn't like me asking if he was OCD. He wanted me to sit down. I'm a little elevated, so I said I prefer to stand. He said to sit down again, and I simply asked if he had a little OCD going on. Crazy. Simply crazy."

We go through double doors down the hallway. I ask about my purse. He says they'll take care of it. We go through a set of locked double doors, and there is the front desk. A bunch of nurses look very busy.

"Here she is," the orderly says. "Okay, we'll take it from here," a young, perky nurse smiles and says. "Okay, Miss April. We have some papers for you to sign."

"I can't read anything without my glasses, and they have my purse up front."

"That's okay," she says with a sinister smile. "It just says this is consent to treat you."

"I don't need medication."

"That's okay. It's just a consent form."

That's okay. That's okay. Okay for her. She's not the

one locked in here. The form looks innocent enough. What I can see of it. So I sign. Anything to get me out of here faster.

I look to my right and see the girl who looks like Julia Roberts. She has a horse shirt on. She looks like she rides horses. She looks scared, but she's just sitting there observing everyone. I walk over and sit next to her.

"I saw you in the intake room. I was in the room two doors down from you. They got you to sign. I wanted to yell in 'Don't do it!'"

"I came here for help. Now I think I made a big mistake."

"Yeah. This is all a mistake. I came here to get evaluated and knew it was a bad sign when the door locked behind me."

The nurse's aide came up to me.

"Okay, Miss April." I hate that, Miss April. Like I'm some kind of kid. Miss April. How condescending. "Follow me."

The perky little aide takes me into a small room.

"First, I need your hair clip," she says smiling. Don't know why she's smiling. I reluctantly take the hair clip from my hair.

"Do you have an underwire bra on?" Strange question, but I'm caught off guard, and I say, "Yes."

"You'll need to remove it, please."

So, I crunch my arms through the armholes in my dress and unhook it and pull it out of my neckline. I feel humiliated. Guess that's the point.

"Next, I need you to jump up and down." I do what I'm asked. This is all so strange. "We'll let you keep your cross on."

"Thank you," I muster. You're God damn right, I will keep my cross on. My angels are here. I can see them, but no one else can. Yea, the cross stays on.

"Okay, you can go back out now," the perky little bitch says.

That was humiliating. Like I was really going to use my bra for some sinister reason.

I go to the front desk and ask, "Can I make an appointment to see the CEO? Who's the CEO? I need to see him, so this whole mistake can be cleared up."

CEO? I need to see him so this whole mistake can be cleared up."

The nurse just looks at me perplexed and ignores me.

Next, an orderly dressed all in white, comes up to me and says, "Let me show you to your room."

I'm anxious and fidgety and really have no choice but to follow him. I talk to him the whole way to the room.

I say, "I'm really not supposed to be here. Do you know the CEO? This is all a mistake, and I really need to leave."

"Ma'am, I'm just doing my job." We continue walking down the long hallway, and it seems like he's moving in slow motion. "Here's your room."

I step in and the first thing I see is a girl lying on a bed. She rolls over and just stares at me.

"Hi, I'm April," I say as I extend my hand out for a handshake.

She softly says, "Hi, I'm Lisa."

Later, I will find out she's terrified of the dark.

The orderly says, "I'll let you two get acquainted. If you need something, just go to the desk."

The room is dismal. No pictures on the walls. Just plain old tan paint. There are two single beds with iron headboards. There's a tan dresser, but I have no need for that as I was locked in here involuntarily and so I only have the clothes I'm wearing. I turn to Lisa and ask, "Why are you in here?"

She quietly tells me, "I was on vacation at Disney with three friends, and I got scared. I'm from Pennsylvania. They didn't know what to do, so they called the cops. The cops then Baker Acted me."

I feel sorry for her as she's this frail little thing.

Later that night when I'm ready to go to sleep, the room light is on. I ask Lisa if I can turn out the light, and she looks at me with sorrowful eyes and says, "I sleep with the lights on because I'm afraid of the dark." God bless her.

That night, I sleep for 14 hours. Guess my little body needs it. Earl, a big black man who was also Baker Acted, says he stopped by my room but saw I was asleep, so he left. Kind of makes me uneasy that he saw me sleeping.

I meet Earl in the courtyard. Every couple of hours, they let us out into the courtyard for 30 minutes. Kind of like caged animals. But a saving grace is that they let you smoke. They only give you two cigarettes, but praise the Lord anyhow.

The first time I meet Earl, he's sitting on a log in the middle of the courtyard with two other black guys, one of them reminding me of Ghandi. I walk over to the log and ask, "Can I sit here?" I have the hood on my black dress up over my head as to look intriguing. Mysterious, if you will.

Earl looks at me and says, "Sit right down, Mama."

I ask Earl what he's in for.

He tells me, "I'm bipolar and on meds. I came here and asked if I could get a refill. The lady asked me how long I've been without my meds, and I said two days. Right away they said Baker Act him. Crazy. I came here for help, and they do this." I can empathize with him. Later, he'll paint my nails for me during "Art Time." I share my story with him and we both agree, this is crazy.

They don't care if you have family obligations or appointments, or even a job. They just seem to enjoy saying, "Baker Act her" or "Baker Act him." And the taking of the cell phone must be so that the outside world doesn't know what's going on inside this crazy house.

It's day two in this madhouse. Earl sees me during courtyard time. He tells me his roommate was standing over him as he woke up. His roommate had a pillow in his hands like a football touchdown sign. Earl said he yelled. He was afraid his roommate was going to smother his face. He made a mad dash for the door and went straight to the front desk and told them what happened. Earl said they took their good 'ole time checking out the incident. Turns out his roommate is Tom. Mild-mannered Tom that I spoke to about his mother. He probably suffers from PTSD and was scared. They probably never did let him call his Mom.

I go to the front desk and ask to see an administrator. I tell the head nurse, "This is all a mistake, and I'd like to speak with an administrator."

She looks at me incredulously. As if I have no rights. She tells me she'll give him the message.

8:00 AM, and it's time for breakfast. We line up like cattle in front of the door between the cafeteria and where they are corralling us. We stand in line waiting. Finally, an orderly comes and takes attendance. Like we are in kindergarten. He unlocks the door, and we all shuffle down the hallway to the cafeteria like little ducklings following their mama. We enter the cafeteria and get in line. The cooks all look like they want to be somewhere else. That's fine, because I'd like to be somewhere else, too. Hard to believe I've been here one day and one sleepless night.

I go through the buffet line. The food doesn't look half bad. It doesn't look half good either. I spy Earl and Lisa at a table. I shuffle off towards their table and sit down. I face myself towards the door, just in case someone goes nuts, and I have to make a mad dash for the door. Talking with Earl, he still cannot believe they Baker Acted him. I can tell Lisa is still scared. 8:30, and it's time to line up, whether you are finished eating or not. The orderly commands us to line up, and he does a head count. This feels like a prison not a therapeutic place.

Out the door and into the hallway as we shuffle back to the locked doors and are corralled inside the prison. We have a little bit of freedom behind the locked doors. There is a room with two tattered couches and a small TV. There's nothing on the walls, just gray paint. There is one plastic plant in the corner. There is a separate coffee room where we are allowed to make ourselves coffee, tea, or hot chocolate. I just want to sit and have a smoke, but I have to wait for courtyard time at 10:00.

I go to the front desk and ask the nurse if I could please see the administrator because this is all a mistake. She said she would check. After courtyard time, the nurse tells me I can see the administrator. She shows me to her office. I smile and thank her. First helpful thing they've done for me in here. I sit down in front of the administrator's desk. I sink into the chair. I suspect this is a power tactic. I tell the administrator what happened and that this is all a mistake.

He looks at me and says, "You can either stay here for three days, or go before the judge and risk having to stay here for a week." Point blank. Three days versus a week to keep your mouth shut. Sounds like injustice to me.

I can sense him getting annoyed with me, so I say, "Three days is enough," and I head out of his office feeling defeated. The feeling you get when you know you just can't win.

2:00, and it's time for games. Guess they call it play therapy. We head down to a small gymnasium with a basketball hoop and tables along the wall. There are coloring sheets with markers and crayons. The "coach" has a basketball and tries to get us interested in shooting hoops. I see Earl painting Lisa's finger nails. I ask him where he learned that, and he says, "Having six sisters, you learn how to do nails."

I ask him if he'd like to do mine next. He finishes with Lisa and then takes my hand and starts filing my nails. I'm feeling pampered, so I guess this game time is therapeutic. But it's us, the ones locked up, that make it that way.

After game time, I go to the lounge, get a cup of coffee, and head into the TV room. I can see the desperation in the eyes of the committed. No one wants to be here.

Day 3 has finally arrived. I ask the nurse at the front desk when I can leave, and she says, "After you meet with the counselor about your exit plan."

Exit plan. Yes, I plan to exit as fast as I can from this hell hole. I ask if I can call my husband, so he can meet me, and she says the phone at the end of the hallway works. I quickly make a bee line towards the phone. I call Mike and I tell him to just come here and get me out of here.

I go to the TV lounge and wait. Wait for my name to be called. Finally, Jeannie, the counselor, calls my name. She directs me to her 6' by 6' cramped office. She asked who my doctor was, then she dialed the phone number and set up an appointment with him. She then went over my medication. Then that was that. She told me I was free to go. Yes, freedom! I went quickly to my room and packed up. I don't want to risk them changing their minds. Yes, freedom!

I go to the front desk to get my wallet and purse, and I'm shocked to see they had my stuff labeled "Mary Showers." That was my mom's name. They didn't even get my name right. They buzz me out, and I quickly head for the double doors down the hallway. I ring the bell, and an orderly buzzes me out. I open the doors as fast as I can, and I see Mike. I hug him but not long, because I'm so afraid they are going to change their minds and keep me in this hell hole of a hospital.

I say, "Quick Mike, let's get out of here."

I go to the parking lot and see my cherry red Mustang convertible. It's calling my name and saying, *please put the top down and let's roll.*

Freedom, yes, sweet, sweet, freedom. And that is my story of three days in a madhouse. Little do I know that in two months, I will spend 11 days being Baker Acted again. But that's a whole other story.

Epilogue

April Showers is a fictitious name based on a true story, my story. I decided to use a pen name because of the all too real stigma associated with mental illness. The real April Showers lives in Central Florida with her husband of 29 years. He is divorcing her because he can't risk losing their house and assets that they've worked their whole lives for. April still has highs where she spends uncontrollably and lows where she's in bed all day. She is on 1.5 mg. Vraylar, 40 mg. Latuda, 50 mg. Pristiq. The medication helps, but it's not a cure all. April finds support at NAMI (National Alliance of the Mentally Ill) meetings, and she attends them regularly.

She is currently working as a Peer Counselor for Lifestream Behavioral Center in Leesburg, Florida. Her goal is to never be Baker Acted again. She has a good support system of four brothers and one sister. She has a small circle of good friends and neighbors, cousins and nieces and nephews that tell her when they see symptoms of the bipolar illness.

April has a therapy dog named Dottie. Dottie helps to regulate April's moods. A dog is a responsibility and unfortunately, sometimes Dottie gets neglected, and April's husband needs to step in.

When the divorce is final, April will be living on her own. She's not sure if she can handle that, but only time will tell. Thank you for reading my story and God Bless.

Favorite Quotes Where I Find Inspiration

Be kinder than necessary, because everyone you meet is fighting some kind of battle.

A sharp tongue can cut your own throat.

If you want your dreams to come true, you must not oversleep.

The best vitamin for making friends ... B1.
The heaviest thing you can carry is a grudge.

One thing you can give and still keep is your word.

One thing you can't recycle is wasted time.

Together may we give our children the roots to grow and the wings to fly.

Never doubt that a small group of thoughtful, committed people can change the world, indeed, it is the only thing that ever has.

In gloomy moods, it's never wise to sit at home and mope. Go out and take a long brisk walk—fresh air creates fresh hope.

We learn 10 percent of what we read, 20 percent of what we hear, 30 percent of what we see, 50 percent of what we see and hear, 70 percent of what we discuss, 80 percent of what we experience, 95 percent of what we teach to others.

April's mother was a poet and wrote the following poem to her on her 43rd birthday:

To April on Her 43rd Birthday
Forty-three is a good age to be,
Right in the middle of Life's symphony,
So dance to the time with a sprightly step,
A lot of good living is there for you yet.

You are a mother, a teacher, a loyal friend,
A wife, a daughter, all roles you can tend.
Take pride in these roles that you live day by day,
You are loved, you are blest as you travel life's way.

(P.S. I was 43 when you were born. 43+43=86)

Goals 2019

Mood Management:

- Goal: Maintain stable mood/Maintain even mood
- Get 7-8 hours of restful sleep every night
- Limit to one serving of a dessert/day
- Two fruit servings/day
- Two vegetable servings/day
- Limit smoking to not more than 10/day
- Stay on meds
- Milk Thistle/ B-vitamin/ NAC each day

Personal Hygiene and Self Care:

- Goal: Improve personal hygiene and attentiveness to self-care
- Brush teeth 2x/day

- Floss once/day
- Use antiperspirant after showering
- Shower every day
- Brush hair every day

Stress:

- Goal: Be able to cope with routine life stressors and take things in stride
- Stretch once/day

Vocational:

- Goal: Paid employment
- One mystery shop/month
- Fill out one Indeed.com application/week.
- Maintain job as Peer Counselor for Lifestream Behavioral Center
- Publish Baker Acted! Three Days in a Madhouse.

Spiritual:

- Goal: Feed my soul
- Say one Our Father and one Hail Mary/day.
- Thank God for all my blessings

My Resume

April Showers
april.showers@hotmail.com

OBJECTIVE: A position where my creativity, talents, and enthusiasm will be utilized for the achievement and enrichment of my colleagues, the organization, and the community.

SUMMARY OF QUALIFICATIONS:

- Six years as an evaluator of customer service in restaurants, hotels, and retail operations.
- Fifteen years certified classroom teaching experience in first, second, third, fifth, and sixth grades. Taught students with IEP's, learning disabilities, and ADHD, as well as general education students.
- Demonstrated leadership abilities as grade-level chair and head of school-wide committees.
- Exceptional performance ratings and the proven ability to be a team-player and accept new challenges as opportunities.

EDUCATION:

- MASTER OF ARTS in ADMINISTRATIVE MANAGEMENT, PUBLIC ADMINISTRATION, University of Maryland (European Division), G.P.A. 3.8
- BACHELOR OF SCIENCE in ELEMENTARY EDUCATION, Kutztown University, Kutztown, PA,

PROFESSIONAL EXPERIENCE:

Independent Evaluator of Customer Service - Performed restaurant, hotel, and retail evaluations for Service with Style, Coyle Hospitality, Data Quest, Regal Hospitality, Buckalew Hospitality, and Customer Impact. July 2012-Present.

Private Tutor - For students ranging in age from first through eighth grades. November 2009-June 2014.

Lead Sales Associate - Retail sales associate for Almost Perfect Furniture. Assisted customers in acquiring housing décor. February 2010-February 2011.

Laubach Adult Literacy Tutor - Taught adults how to read utilizing the Laubach Way to Reading program. December 2011-June 2014.

Third Grade Teacher - The Villages Charter Intermediate School, The Villages, FL. August 2004-July 2009. Duties and Accomplishments:

- Grade-Level Chairperson for the third grade team
- Key member of the K-12 science curriculum committee
- Organized and ran the Lego, chess, and beginning German after-school clubs
- Mentor for two first year teachers

Private Kindergarten Tutor - For the daughter of Dr. Normarie Albino, Pediatrician, The Villages, FL. September 2001-May 2002.

Sixth Grade Teacher - Department of Defense Dependents Schools, Sollars Elementary School, Misawa Air Base, Japan. August 1995-June 1997. Duties and Accomplishments:

- Exceptional Performance Rating for school years 1995/96 and 1996/97
- Cash Performance Award for exceeding performance in all areas for school year 1995/96
- Grade-Level Chairperson for the sixth grade team
- Mentor/Peer Coach for first year teacher

First Grade Teacher - Department of Defense Dependents Schools, Upwood Elementary School, RAF Upwood, England. August 1993-June 1995. Duties and Accomplishments:

- Exceptional Performance Rating for school years 1993/94 and 1994/95
- Cash Performance Awards for exceeding performance in all duty areas for school years 1993/94 and 1994/95
- Primary Grade-Level Chairperson for the primary team and specialists. 15 member team

Second Grade Teacher - Department of Defense Dependents Schools, Atterberry Elementary School, Frankfurt, Germany. August 1992-June 1993. Duties and Accomplishments:

- Exceptional Performance Rating for school year 1992/93
- Chairperson of the School's Early Childhood Education Committee
- Chairperson of the School's Advisory Committee.

First Grade Teacher - Department of Defense Dependents Schools, Nuernberg Elementary School, Nuernberg, Germany. August 1990-June 1992. Duties and Accomplishments:

- Coordinated school events that utilized our unique host country setting
- Active member of the school's discipline committee.

Fifth Grade Teacher - Round Hill Elementary School, Loudoun County Public Schools, Virginia. August 1988-June 1990. Duties and Accomplishments:

- Chairperson for school's Self-Study Steering Committee
- Developed research proposal on flash cards versus computers in math fact drill practice by fifth grade students
- Directed the school play, *Dickens' A Christmas Carol*

Volunteer Work:

- Stanton-Weirsdale ES Parent Center Volunteer Coordinator in conjunction with the Success by Six initiative of the United Way of Marion County, Florida. October 2003-June 2004.
- Old Faithful Inn, Yellowstone National Park, Wyoming. Initial point of contact at the Information Desk of the Old Faithful Inn. Utilizing park programs, training courses, and all other

available resources, I recommended and planned activities for guests. July 1997–October 1997

- St. Theresa's Soup Kitchen Server, Belleview, FL. June 2000–June 2001
- Public Policy Institute of Marion County, FL. Helped complete study of youth violence in Marion County, FL, and issue a report to the citizens of the county. September 1999–April 2000

Interests: Family, Traveling, Biking, Reading, Mystery Shopping

About the Author

April grew up in Whitehall, Pennsylvania, a middle-class suburb of Allentown, Pennsylvania. She graduated from Kutztown University with a Bachelor's of Elementary Education. She taught fifth grade for two years at Round Hill ES, Virginia. She then got hired by the Department of Defense Dependents Schools (DoDDS). She and her husband lived in Nuernberg and Frankfurt, Germany, for three years, then moved to RAF Upwood, England. She taught first grade there and completed her Masters in Public Administration through the University of Maryland. After two years, she and her husband got reassigned to Misawa Air Base, Japan. She taught first and sixth grades there.

After seven years of being overseas, April and her husband took fun jobs at Yellowstone National Park and worked at the Old Faithful Inn. After working a season there, they moved to Central Florida to start a family. Their son was born in 1999. April decided to be a stay-at-home mom, which is a misnomer because you are never at home when being a stay-at-home mom. She stayed home with her son for five years.

When her son started kindergarten, she went to work at The Villages Charter School as a third grade teacher. She did that for five years, but then had a nervous breakdown and was fired July, 2009. It wasn't a pretty picture. She had experienced a suicidal depression in 2008 after her sister died at the age of 58; her mom found out she had cancer, and her best friend had breast cancer. Teaching was stressful, and she fell into a dark depression, but then several months later, she bounced up into a mania. Her principal and colleagues missed the warning signs, and ultimately, she got fired while in a mania. She called her principal Hitler, and she had to be removed by the cops.

Her family and friends encouraged her to seek psychiatric help. Without a job means you're without health insurance. So, she made an appointment in 2011 with The Centers, the public mental health clinic in Ocala, Florida. Her husband went with her to the initial visit.

April hoped and prayed the diagnosis would just be a thyroid problem, but after listening intently to April's history, the Nurse Practitioner diagnosed April as Bipolar 1, the more severe type of bipolar disorder. She was put on Depakote. At her three-month check-up, her liver enzymes were elevated. She was pulled off of Depakote and put on Seroquel. For the next couple of years, April went on just about every medication for the treatment of Bipolar 1 disorder. She swung through depressions and manias, which seemed to follow a seasonal pattern. She became discouraged and was Baker Acted in 2013 for three days in August and 11 days in November.

She saw numerous psychiatrists and even participated in an Abilify study for the injectable form. She is currently in recovery. She was working as a second grade teacher in a Florida public school, but was then moved involuntarily to first grade, and those little five- and six-year-olds ate her alive. She resigned November 2, 2018, for her mental health. She then had a hypo-manic episode in December 2018. Her husband asked her for a divorce, so he could at least save their assets that they worked their whole lives to achieve.

She is currently a Peer Counselor for Lifestream Behavioral Health in Leesburg, Florida. She takes her meds religiously and makes sure she sleeps on a regular basis. She is hopeful about the future and prays every day for the strength to tend to all her life's roles.

What People are Saying:

"Your story is intriguing and certainly draws the reader in. The imagery is evocative…you have a really good way of capturing the almost manic stream of conscious. Colorful and compelling. A poignant read." Mary Flynn, author of Disney's *Secret Sauce*.

"A unique story with action and a power play between staff and clients." Kim Autry, bipolar mood disorder patient.

"It felt like I was there. Very eerie." Lynn Tretter, lifelong friend.